THE PARK [illegible]

by Sandra Iversen

In My Community

Content Vocabulary

knee pad

pond

seat

skater

statue

You can skate on the ice in the park nearby. What time of year do you think it is?

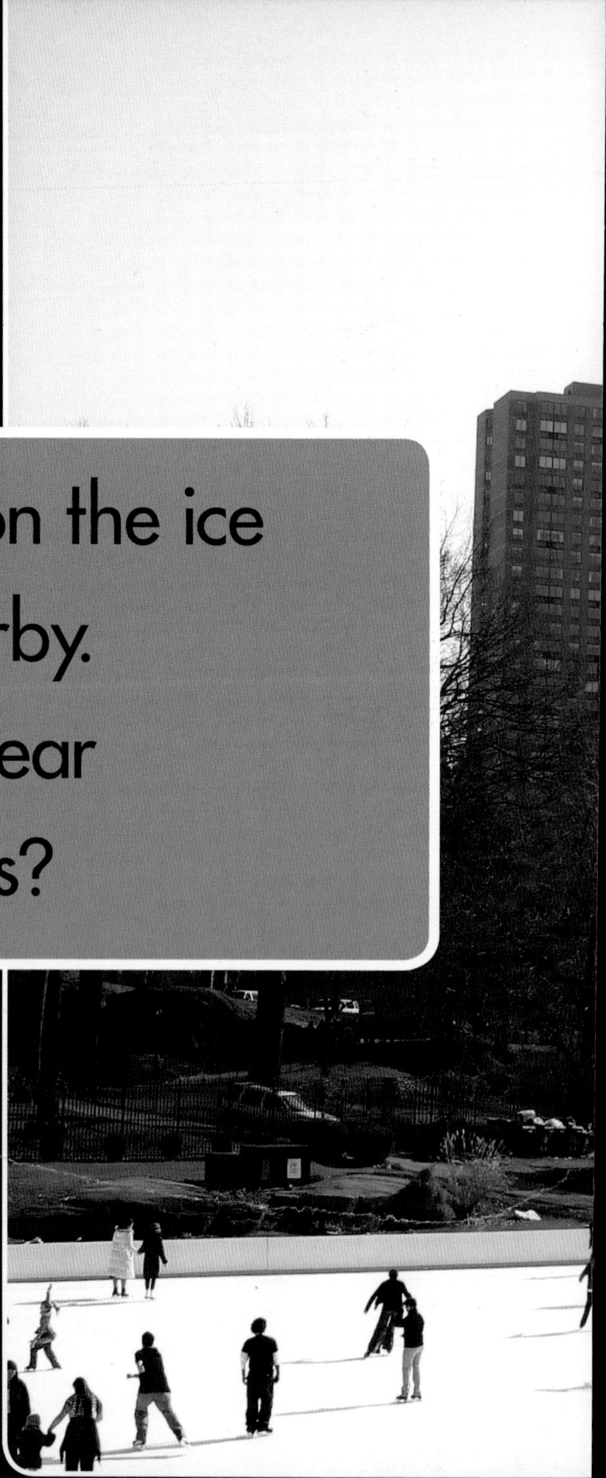

ice
skater

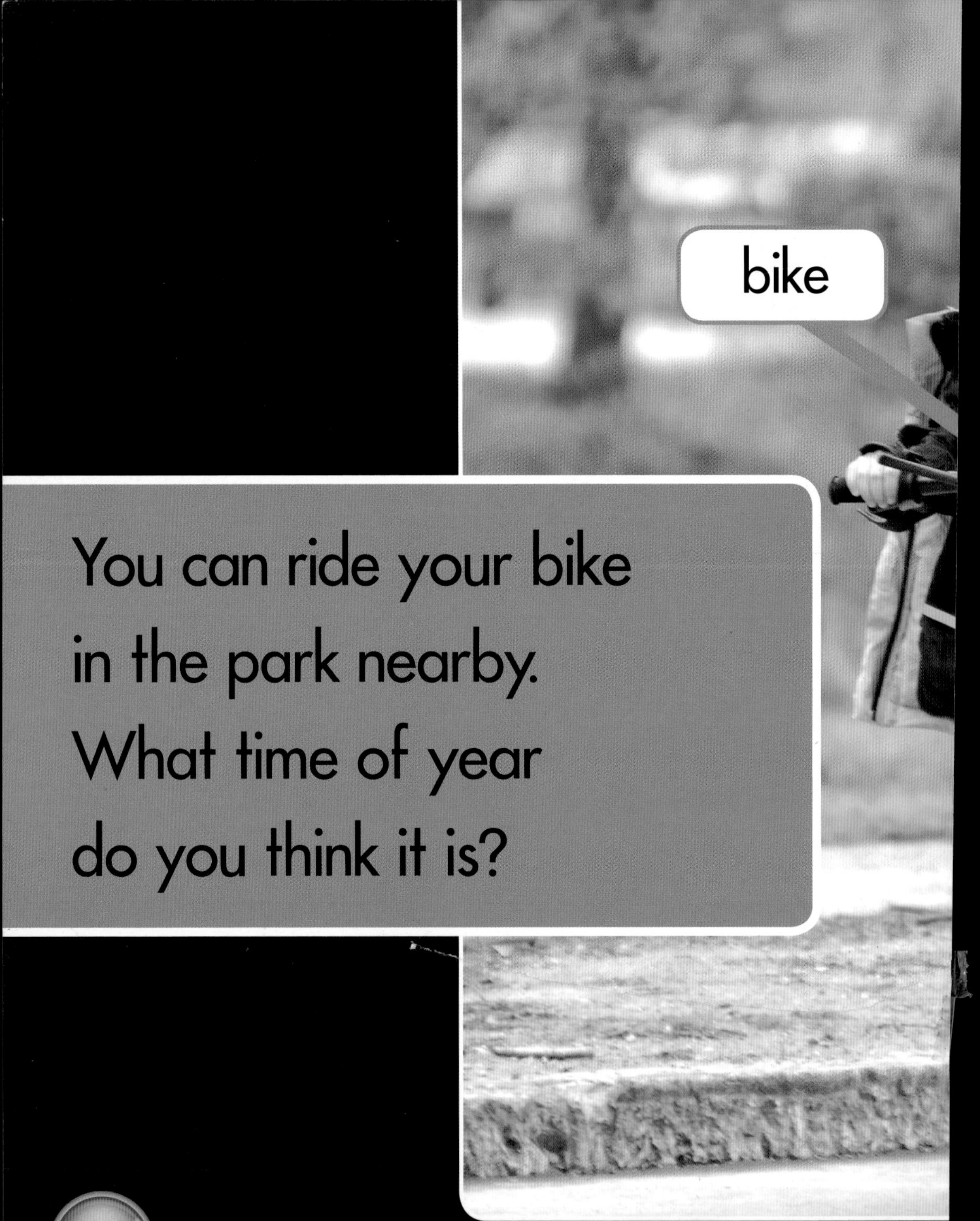

You can ride your bike in the park nearby. What time of year do you think it is?

knee pad

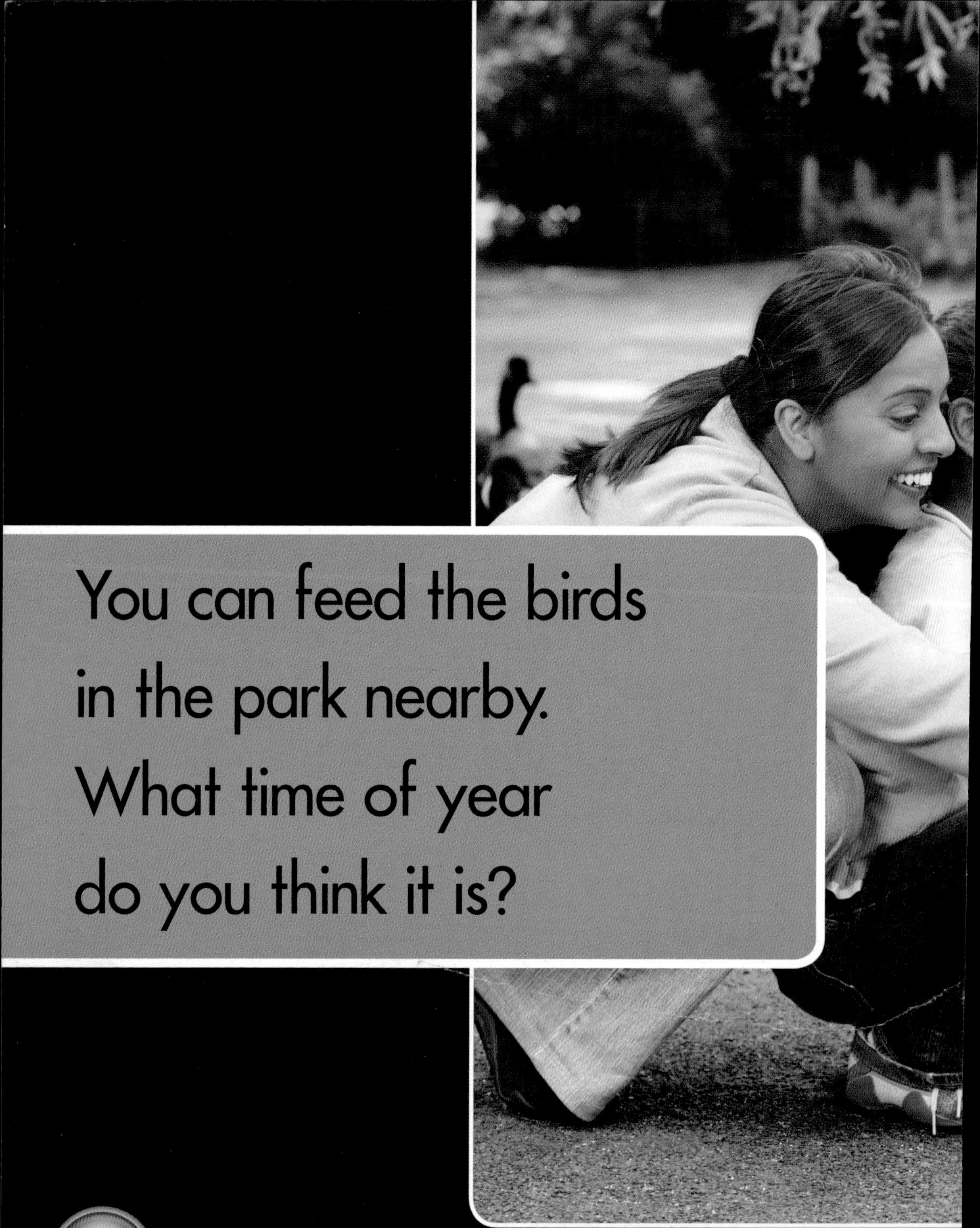

You can feed the birds in the park nearby. What time of year do you think it is?

birds
bread

You can sit in the sun
in the park nearby.
What time of year
do you think it is?

fountain
statue

This is the park nearby.
What time of year
do you think it is?

pond
seat

FROM SPRING TO WINTER

Visual literacy: Relationship Chart

Extra Vocabulary

building

gull

jacket

leaves

path